REALITY, MYTHS AND THE

50 *years*

OF A WOMAN

Dally Hernandez

Cover designed by Laura Antonioli.

Paper back ISBN: 978-1-63877-651-2
eBook ISBN: 978-1-63877-654-3
Hard Cover ISNB: 978-1-63877-645-1

This book is dedicated to all women who will one day be 50 years old, to those who are past 50 and to all women who are living this precious age, because they deserve all the love and respect in the world.

To all the women who are part of my life, you have been my inspiration.

Table of Contents

Introduction

The world needs women, brave women, women who decide, women who fight, women who know how to approach life with optimism; the world needs each and every woman, because that's who we are. The world is changing and with it, the way a woman acts. Throughout history women have played different roles, each of them of great weight and importance. The false concept of being weak and fragile has changed with modern society, and women have shown through their actions that this concept is completely wrong. Even so, we continue to fight to prove that we are emotional, but also strong and enterprising.

Hence the importance of this book. To show women that just because you are now entering the age of 50, you don't stop being the wonderful person that celebrates the excitement of life, that expresses her joy for the victories not yet experienced, and you can still fight for your dreams until they become reality. To teach you, that there is more to life than making others happy. Life is designed to find happiness within yourself.

The beginning

"It can be a morning like any other morning in any given month, it can be a night like any other night in a random year. Everything around us and what we have in our lives can be almost the same when we discover that we are the ones who decide what can be really different."

It was only a few years ago when this story, that is rarely talked about but felt by many, began. On one of those mornings when the sun seemed to warm Sara's hands, no one could have suspected that the sun wasn't shining inside her that day. She went out in her red dress, orange almost, to drink her long awaited coffee, nothing different from what she did almost every morning. She went out to explore the forest that she called enchanted, not necessarily because it had anything special but because she loved getting lost in the high branches, swaying in the wind, and yes, even listening to the sounds and whispers of the creatures that ran and flew through that magical place. It was on that morning, that she discovered nothing in her surroundings made her happy but she didn't know why. After diving into the silence of her own being and trying to find thousands of answers to questions she had never asked herself before, she discovered that all human beings need to find a space in their own world. A place where you can connect the silence you have inside, with that special something everyone talks about, but very few are able to see.

It was on that morning, which was like many other mornings, that her world took an unexpected turn and then she was ready to enter her house and face life, a life that might not be perfect but definitely not the worst of lives either. She understood that there were other beings in this space who really needed help, dreams, and reasons to start walking through unknown paths.

"Come in," she said to her neighbor Rosa.

"Are you OK?" Rosa asked.

"Yes, just a bit confused, the coffee is cold, shall we make a new one?" she asked.

They returned together to her favorite place in the house, where she was able to connect with her soul, where she felt the wonders of this space she shared with herself. Her heart was pounding as she thought that her own being was capable of going beyond the imaginable.

"Are you sure you're OK? I feel like you are so far away, distant from everything right now." Rosa said to her.

"Yes, neighbor, don't worry, it's just that the smell of the Earth and mountains reminds me of the little girl full of hopes and dreams that I was. Don't you feel it too when you sit here?"

"Yes, you're right, I often think that life... *(there was silence)* ... didn't turn out like I wanted, I didn't fight for my dreams as a woman, for the desire to be someone with my own decisions... Oh well Sara, what can I do about it now?!"

"Who knows, Rosa, life may still surprise you and make the universe connect with your thoughts, making you relive feelings you might think are already dead."

"Well, who knows... you're very existential today, come on, let's make some more coffee and talk about our dreams."

They went back to the kitchen and made coffee, then came back and sat down to talk just like they did most mornings.

When a woman reaches a certain age, it's very difficult to admit, she could enter an existential change, not an identity crisis, but starting to experience different feelings and see life as she has not seen it before. Every woman reaches an age when her thoughts and feelings start to take different paths.

One day without any warning everything changes, you don't get any signals or messages, the change comes and brings experiences that you haven't lived before, what you saw with gentleness you now see from another angle, and life becomes a constant challenge in which you become the protagonist of your own novel, and nobody else but you can decide what role you're going to play in your new world.

It all began with the arrival of the half century, as they usually call it. Sara looked at herself in the mirror and noticed that her face seemed to be the same, but in reality it wasn't, she wanted to walk until she found a sense of freedom, a desire for the air that was caressing her face to be stronger. For a moment she thought that this could only be happening to her. She decided to be quiet and to join in with everyone around her.

"That's life", a common phrase which had nothing to do with Sara, the truth is that she didn't even say it out loud, but in order not to enter into another kind of conflict, she simply repeated it inside herself and kept quiet. But on that morning she became her new self. On that morning, that common phrase didn't have any room in her mind any more.

Talking is what helps us, talking to other women who feel the same way and are not able to talk, due to fear, taboo, lack of determination, comfort, or not believing that the same thing is happening to others.

Talking to other women, gives us more confidence to open up about our own experiences. Half a century arrives, the "Fabulous 50's" that nobody wants to talk about, the age many people think, *"I'm old"* or *"...well I have lived a lot...".* 50 arrives and what happens? Well, a lot happens! You look in the mirror and discover that as if by magic, your body, your face and above all, how you see life has changed. The age comes when you value yourself, respect yourself, many inner changes begin to reveal themselves to you. You need to talk about it, you need to say what you have, what you think, and with this wonderful age you begin to have dreams. In addition to those dreams, comes some kind of depression. Well maybe that is not the exact word, but there are definitely changes in your nervous system as well as hormonal changes, which are purely normal in the body. The wonderful thing, is that it comes without warning, it's another year, but it's not really another year, it's the year where everything comes at the same time, a year where you have to rediscover yourself, when the woman you were is no longer there. You want to say to other women *"...you are not alone, ...there are a lot of us, ...it is human, we feel and there is nothing wrong in expressing what you feel, ...others may not understand, for reasons beyond them, but we are not crazy and there is no need to self-medicate".*

Sara began to recall a bit of history. In the 60's when a woman reached half a century of age, she would experience a high level of depression and due to lack of information, many would resort to suicide, or were isolated in mental hospitals.

She recalled the case of a very famous lady in her town who used to walk the streets... *Lucia, they called her. One day, that woman was no longer who she was, and her life turned like the wind, she moved aimlessly through streets and alleys, barefoot. She had lost sense of what everyone considered normal. She lived in a world created by her, always bare footed, dancing and spinning in the wind, with her white gown, covered in dirt and her smile tinged with light. That woman was looked at by everyone with pity, but she was perhaps the happiest because her world was the one she had decided to live in.*

The lack of information keeps hitting us in the face, the lack of communication turns us into cold beings. We want to believe that we are strong, but what gives us strength? What gives us the appearance of strength? Our children, our spouses and our loved ones have to understand that we are fragile simple beings that can be strong, but we can also collapse with just one look. We come to this world to give color and joy, we are independent unique beings, and when we reach a certain age all the planets come together and we start to rethink our lives. We are not crazy, we have to talk, meet with other women and friends. We have to dance, laugh, scream, walk and let the wind hit us in the face to feel alive.

That morning Sara decided to break her silence and talk to her coffee neighbor, as she used to call her. That morning, everything started to change, and as she talked to more women, she decided to say "*...I am not well ...I feel sad and I want to cry*". She cried a river of tears until her eyes dried up but when she composed herself as she always did, her chest was free of sorrows.

"Cry, my friend, you have to cleanse your soul", Rosa told her.

That is how the lives of these two women in their 50s began to change as they decided to share life experiences that they had not shared before. Sara began to talk to other women and share her experiences. There was a before and after in their lives, there were phrases like *"no I don't want to"*, *"no it doesn't matter"*, *"I am fine"*, that became *"I am not crazy, it is normal"*, *"it is part of our body, to change and yes, to accept it"*, *"our anatomy changes and it is okay"*, *"we cannot always be firm"*, *"we get depressed because it is hard to accept that we are no longer 20, but we refuse to let ourselves fall"*, and *"there are so many women just like us, we simply need to live as life presents itself to us"*.

Every moment of our life is filled with colors, but we are the ones that decide which colors to wear. Remembering Lucia, the town lady, made Sara think about herself and her desires. What is the point of always being there to please others? No point absolutely. Life is not about making others happy when we are not able to be happy ourselves. Although there are those who think that happiness does not exist, I still want to think that it does, and it is created by yourself, you decide who gets in and who doesn't.

Breaking the silence was a new beginning for Sara, as well as many other women who dared to stop pretending that what they were projecting was an appearance of happiness within their lives as mothers, wives, sisters, businesswomen and more. No one dares to talk about what happens when you reach 50, but it's something very real, and the lack of truth about the subject, if not discussed, can risk becoming something unbearable.

Sara knew this would be the beginning of a new chapter in her life. That same day, after a long and deep conversation with her husband, who supported her unconditionally, Sara knew she had to be heard by other women as she put her strength to the test.

How it started

"The door is open, now only you decide if you want to enter."

We all know when there's something bothering us, it's something we feel, nobody notices it, and most of the time we do not let others perceive it the way we are feeling it. We have the tendency to remain passive or conformed, even when we are not at ease. We go on days, years and quite possibly a lifetime. Many women die without having experienced independence or decision making in their lives.

"You have to do it Rosa, you have to make a decision based on your feelings, what's the point of living in a relationship in which you're not even allowed to have an opinion? Are you happy?" asked Sara.

"I don't know Sara, I've given up on understanding happiness. There are only certain moments when I connect with myself... Well, it doesn't matter. He gives me everything, a roof, food, he takes care of my children, what more can I ask for, right? It's true, my hopes and youthful dreams were different, but life can change and nothing really happens... you end up in a different way, then you realize that your dreams were just that, dreams."

"Absolutely not, you're wrong. It is never too late to start being you, to realize that there is more to life. Aren't you important? Don't you want to feel free, alive with desires? Take a good look at yourself, you are still young, you have something to fight and live for."

Both friends were lost in a cloud of uncertainty and doubts, even though Sara had a clearer idea now, her sorrow for Rosa conflicted her. She worried about how to help her and the thought of how to make her wake up, distressed her even more.

It is difficult, so to speak, to wake up from a reality that seems normal to us, especially when we constantly refuse to see our own truth. It's as if everything that other people can see, is a lie to us, we only see our own version of existence. It is necessary to take a step back and observe life from another angle, as a spectator.

The awakening

*"Life is a movie that you can enjoy if you play
a role other than the protagonist and have the
courage to watch it."*

It all began two years ago, when for some twist of fate and without any planning Sara moved to her ideal city, to the place where she had always wanted to live, the place of her dreams, where a stillness surrounded sunsets and warmth caressed the dawn. There, she met lots of people that from that moment on became part of her life, among them, her neighbor Rosa, who quickly became a friend. They chatted daily and shared a cup of coffee almost every morning. More than that, they had many points of view in common. The only thing they did not talk about was how to advocate for their dreams, how to fight for what they had always wanted.

Rosa, who was a few years older, had already passed her 50th and saw nothing extraordinary in it. It was simply an age, one more wrinkle to worry about. Her desires had lost their meaning and her aspirations were simply, according to her, part of an immature girl's illusion. Her reality was quite different. She had been married to the same man she met when she was 15 years old, she had two children and didn't work because it was her husband's job to support her and cover her needs, in case she had any. She always had a look of sadness on her face, but denied it. Her intention to justify her life always accompanied her. Rosa wasn't the type of woman who would stop her life just to start again with her head held high, no, she was the type of woman who would keep her head down and continue as if nothing had happened.

"Sometimes I think my children left because I don't know how to say no to Robert," she said to Sara, "You don't know how many times I have wondered if it was my fault that they left."

"Of course my friend, but it's nothing like that. Children leave, it is the natural law of life. Didn't we leave? They have to live their lives and grow up."

"Yes, that part I understand. But do you recall that George left after that fight with Robert and Nina left overnight?"

"Yes, I remember, but that's just how it happened, don't go looking for reasons where there are none. Boys wait for the slightest neglect to say I'm leaving and that's it. That's how they are Rosa."

Silence returned to their empty souls. Both of them immersed in their own world, looking for answers to so many heartaches that tormented them. Sara had her own moments of regret, she remembered her trip to Spain, she had left her children alone for the first time. She had missed them, many things happened during that trip. Her troubles, her resolutions, the way John reacted when her eldest son decided to start his new life with his girlfriend. Those things made her live in a state of shock, that despite the positive atmosphere she now had around her, still weighed heavily on her heart.

Two years had passed since she decided to live in her enchanted place and her 50th birthday finally came, half century lived, suddenly all those nightmares that tormented her life became more evident without even expecting it. It was as if they had knocked on the door and entered unannounced. It was precisely then, without any warning, a torrent of tears that shook her bones started to flow, she could not stop. Those were the tears she had not cried during her life for fear of not being strong or positive. She decided to drown all those sorrows in her tears so she could wipe them away and start over.

It was then, that her 50th birthday became an event not previously celebrated. In that moment, her troubles chose another place to take shelter. Courage took over and made it very clear that all doors were going to open and connect her with a new version of herself.

While my memory exists

"When our memory fails us, our dreams will still be our driving force."

Life likes to play hide and seek with its challenges, you think everything is already planned and suddenly BAM! Everything changes; that's when the challenges begin, you search and search for a little opening where you think you will see clearly and suddenly, everything closes forcing you to start all over again until you choose a path and stop playing, or give up and keep the game going.

Giving up was never part of Sara's destiny, however, because no one dared to talk about what many women go through, she felt uneasy. Why are women so afraid to say *"I'm depressed"*, *"I'm panicking"*, *"I feel like the world is falling apart"*?

That's how one day, Sara decided to write her story, which is a story that any woman could be living and there is nothing wrong with that. It is the product of a hormonal change that occurs in every woman, sometimes earlier than others. At some point in our lives, it knocks on our doors, and enters unnoticed but it's up to you if it stays.

How could she forget that 31st of December when her world closed in front of her and without consolation or explanation she broke down in tears. She knew John was a good husband and that he loved her madly, but her life and her feelings were in crisis. Not his, but hers, not the love she had for him, but the emotions she felt in all of those years that were silenced accompanied her like a faithful friend. She blamed herself for not having done more when fate played one of its games. The years in which she was surrounded by people who loved her, she felt alone.

No one can imagine how important mental exercise is. To sit in front of the sea and enjoy the breeze that caresses and touches your spirit. No one should take for granted a gesture that may reach someone unexpectedly. No one knows the effect of a kiss until they taste it, nor the taste of honey until it slowly passes down your throat, no one knows how bitter a goodbye can be until they see their child leave forever. Every fragment of our lives is marked by an experience.

That moment was Sara's first taste of this experience. She had never felt anything like it, she had never experienced loneliness accompanied by fear.

That January, Sara shared a few words with another woman who used to visit Rosa. But for reasons of life itself, Sara did not talk about any subject in depth until that very day when she decided to exchange this existential experience with her. It was then that Sara understood, she was not alone. This feeling had been experienced by other women, some of whom had even had to seek professional help and many of them were on medication.

One thing that had always bothered Sara was the idea of being on medication, it was something she didn't really like or agree with. It is known that medicines can create some kind of dependency and Sara is one of those people who prefers all-natural remedies, but there are times in life, and especially moments like these, where medicines play a very important role. Of course, mental exercises are an essential part of this process and can be the best allies.

"Let's start to remember high school, and let's run with our minds through the streets where we used to go and with who we shared that time," said Sara to her friend Rosa.

"Oh yes, I remember the smell of the sea and how its breeze would make me jump out of bed on July mornings when my sisters would run around the house looking for the best shoes to wear to school."

"In my town it was different, we went out in the middle of the day to have ice cream and when it rained we got wet without fear of thunder, we walked through the flooded streets of that little town with so much joy that not even the rain made us stop."

"What beautiful times we live in Sara. Different places, but with the same taste of enjoyment."

"We should write the dates we lived happily on this stone, then we're going to look at it again in 10 years, what do you think?" said Sara, excited about her idea.

"I love it", replied Rosa with great joy.

They were forging a unique bond between them, a connection that would last through the years. They were writing down something that their memories could not erase.

Seeking answers

"Believing that we have the answers to everything in life is a big mistake, God is the one who guides our steps and we owe it to him."

We tend to question everything as human beings, we are always looking for an explanation to every episode in our lives. Whenever something happens to us, even the smallest thing, we try to connect with another being, we take our thoughts to a space where we meet our inner self. We connect with God.

When I mention God, I mean it! On that morning when Sara put on her red (almost orange) dress, she was certain that God was listening her. In the course of her days everything around her was going to start to have color, because her inner self desired it, longed for it and projected it. Her decisions were going to help other women.

From the moment she spoke to her neighbor, a force greater than herself was driving her on. How many women exist in this world who are not ready to share their feelings for the simple fear of thinking that what they feel may be wrong, for fear of making mistakes or being judged?

What difference does it make? This is an issue for every woman, we are all touched in some way by the so-called mid-life crisis, but why call it a crisis? Does anyone know how many years of bravery a woman goes through without anyone noticing? Obviously not! How many sleepless nights a woman spends on her children, on her parents and her husband? How many internal tears do women cry every second of their lives, when they are certain that everything is not exactly rosy?

Do their life partners, those who manage to live together longer than fate predicts, know how much anguish dwells in their bodies and minds? Of course they do not. Every woman is designed to carry the weight of those around her on her shoulders, and to wake up every morning with the commitment that she will make everyone around her happy. In the subconscious of every woman a commitment to life is created, somehow formed by her ancestors and passed down through generations to be sure that all those around her will always be safe. This is how God makes it possible for every woman to light up her days, and for each one to feel the joy of fulfilling her mission in life.

The crisis has come

"...and so out of the blue you came along to calm our anxieties..."

Sara knew that this was just the beginning of a long road, she knew that Rosa did not fully understand the message and was not ready to fight for herself yet, just like many other women. Not all women are aware of their role in this great journey we decided to embark on together.

Sofia, Sara's younger sister, was always conscious of her role in the journey, unlike other women, she faced her emotions and avoided tears, somehow taking refuge in long trips where sex ruled every dark corner of her being. She was not in her fifties yet and was certain her own crisis would come a little differently.

She had always lived life in her own way; when she was seventeen she had to face many tasteless things alone, and had learned to fill her streets with stones she painted herself to give color to her sunrises. Her children became her strength and driving force, she even created a shield that only she could use to protect them, even from the wind. Who knows when the impatience of age will come upon her? Maybe her cycle will be more colorful and less intense, but it will still come and she will have the strength to fill it, this time with flowers so that her streets have a different meaning.

Sara thought of Lola, John's friend, who so often used her armor of roses to take refuge in solitude, her crisis was marked by the death of her life partner, she stood by his side until his last moments, she cared for him like no one else. No one knew that she was going through her existential crisis, she had not had a single second of pleasure. What did everyone see? A strong and serene woman, with firm steps and a smile on her face, a woman who looked ahead with an illusion of perfection that did not exist, until the touch of death arrived to take her husband. Though we seem to expect it, death always arrives without warning. Life had always been a great challenge, but her inner struggle and her new awakening, made her start living and transforming her mornings of uncertainty and loneliness. She battled to overcome depression, despite her numerous reasons, she rediscovered sex and pleasure. She took up old dreams and although with delay, started her journey through a new decade. Lola enjoyed her evening dinners and her colorful and sensual outfits that Sara had bought for her first steps into the dating world, as they call it because of her late start.

Women in the middle of their 50's have very different experiences, each one with her own colors and fears. Until then, none of them had ever dared to speak out, to confess their sorrows or their worries. When Sara entered her great crisis, each one of them shared details of their experiences, how they felt strengthless, tired of fighting, depressed, each one revealed what they had hidden for the simple reason of not knowing if they were the only ones going through the same existential conflict.

How could so many atrocities committed against women over 50 been avoided for centuries? Lack of information. Everything starts to happen at once and you have to take care of your body, your soul, the food, the joys, the company, the illusions have to be renewed, everything becomes a challenge because you have reached full maturity.

"You become a wonderful woman, full of flavors and well-defined realities. You start to live a new phase but you don't quite know how to do it," said Eva, a friend of Sara's with whom she used to have afternoon lunches once or twice a month. They called it lunch meetings for the soul.

Eva was a very prepared and smart woman, always ready to protect her children in the most noble way she could find, her decisions were not always accurate as she could not be in control of everything around her, even though she believed she was; it was hard for her to understand that our children think very differently from us, and we still have to respect and love them to the point of going above our principles. After she turned 50, Eva became very sensitive and gave in to some insecurity as well. She took medication to cope with the whole world that was suddenly coming down on her. Eva and Sara had a nice friendship, although they didn't always agree on their points of view. Their conversations were always deep and they could discuss all topics without any arguments or prejudices.

"It's a myth Sara", said Eva "sex is still intense and it doesn't change at all, mature doesn't mean old, you'll see..." they laughed a lot on this subject as Sara had many questions with the arrival of age 50.

Important things always come from moments of crisis, changes are usually forever, but some may be an asset for all women. It is necessary to seek help if needed, this will help calm your anxieties. When you understand that all women face this stage in their lives, you will also know that talking about it gives us the strength to continue.

We are what we choose

"How many roads yet without paths, how many ponds yet without memories, how many dewdrops dry on the sand, how many words..."

Hope is what keeps us going, women need projects, human beings need reasons to live, but women need inspiration.

Sara kept thinking about how she would help other women, after a long study, several nights of reading and various conversations with the women who adorned her soul, she discovered the beauty of each one and decided to find the right way to help them.

Her mother was so right; in one of their morning chats she told her "women at 50 are completely whole - it's the ideal age, enjoy it, you'll see".

Sara, who was only 20 years old, told her, "You are not old, you are perfect mother."

How much can be avoided in this life if you shower a woman with compliments, if you admire her strength to love, if you protect her feelings and keep her worries safe? Only women know what their families really need, they can harbor in their breasts the warmth of memories.

Reaching 50 is a challenge for many and a hope for others. The half century is nothing more than the beginning of new hopes, it represents the accumulated experience, but this time dressed in blue with the reflections of the moon, since you can see everything from a stronger angle. Life finally manages to give you the right words to conquer the universe. Now, use the right weapons and don't let the nights become challenges with no escape. Dance, talk, sing the song that inspires you, let the sun light up your mornings, let the wind touch your whole being with its wings. Look for dreams and projects in which you are the protagonist of your own novel.

"Don't live in that sad world", said Sara that ordinary morning to her friend Rosa, "throw yourself into happiness and be yourself, look inside you to find what makes you pulsate".

"I promise I will Sara, I just need time to think and process everything you have told me. Someday I will hear the rain dancing on my window again and the rays of sunlight wishing to take refuge in my soul".

Sara and Rosa made a solidarity pact between friends. They agreed to share a day for the soul, to enjoy their mornings together with a cup of coffee and to meet for an occasional sunset to say goodbye to the sun.

You can achieve everything you set your mind to, be consistent, keep going, there is no need to hurry, just don't stop. We as women have the power to reach the clouds, we simply cannot deviate from the path. We shall not have to please others constantly, sometimes it is necessary to say "... *another time*", "... *later*", "... *me first*".

When you turn 50, remember what your mother told you, "*Life begins now, what you had before was just practice.*"

That is wisdom! Life is giving you the steps, and what happens is that we do not look where we step and we fall without warning on the same path. At 50 you reach the age in which you decide your steps, so use the previous experience and learn to step with the firmness of a mature woman, without fear of being wrong since you have already made mistakes in the past. Choose and do not look back, overcome your worries and face the depression that you know is part of a hormonal process and will be temporary as you cannot allow anything negative to define your life. Fight woman! Challenge yourself!

"I don't know if tomorrow will pass and erase our great memories, that's why today I dress myself with this coat that burns as I conquer the world that opens its doors by your side."

www.ingramcontent.com/pod-product-compliance
Lightning Source LLC
Chambersburg PA
CBHW072329270726
48658CB00016B/2162